MONDAY MORNING
ATHEIST

ORDERING INFORMATION:

Visit www.WorkLife.org for more resources.

Friends — Coworkers — Small Groups
Networks — Churches — Business

MONDAY MORNING

ATHEIST

Why You Switch God OFF at Work

Doug Spada & Dave Scott

WorkLife™ Press

Monday Morning Atheist

Copyright © 2014 by Doug Spada

All rights reserved.

ISBN: 978-0-9839628-0-9

Published by WorkLife™ Press

www.MondaySwitch.com

WorkLife™ is a registered Trademark of WorkLife, Inc.

Printed in United States of America

Second Edition 2014

Cover design by Dale Partridge. Book design by Megan Lane Designs. Production by Suzann Beck, BeckHaus Design, Inc.

Scripture quotations marked (NIV) are taken from the Holy Bible, New International Version®, NIV®. Copyright © 1973, 1978, 1984 by Biblica, Inc.™ Scripture quotations marked (NIRV) are taken from the Holy Bible, New International Reader's Version®. NIV®. Copyright © 1995, 1996, 1998 by Biblica, Inc.™ Both used by permission of Zondervan. All rights reserved worldwide. www.zondervan.com. Scripture quotations marked (The Message) are taken from THE MESSAGE. Copyright © by Eugene H. Peterson 1993, 1994, 1995, 1996, 2000, 2001, 2002. Used by permission of NavPress Publishing Group. Scripture quotations marked (NASB) are taken from the New American Standard Bible®, Copyright © 1960, 1962, 1963, 1968, 1971, 1972, 1973, 1975, 1977, 1995 by The Lockman Foundation. Scripture quotations marked (Amplified) are taken from the Amplified® Bible, Copyright © 1954, 1958, 1962, 1964, 1965, 1987 by The Lockman Foundation. Both used by permission. www.Lockman.org. Scripture quotations marked (NLT) are taken from the Holy Bible, New Living Translation, copyright © 1996, 2004, 2007 by Tyndale House Foundation. Used by permission of Tyndale House Publishers. All rights reserved.

This book is dedicated to the working person

who wonders if his or her work day

really matters to God.

Table of Contents

The Switch!

A note to you, the worker:

If you've ever walked into a dark building at night, you might have found it confusing, and—admit it—maybe even a little scary. Now think of your life at work, spiritually, as that same dark building. Many of us are moving through our work weeks in much the same way: unsure of where we're heading, often anxious about our circumstances, feeling alone, and rightfully concerned that we may be hurt by something up ahead that we can't see.

How did this happen? Well, our research shows that most of us have switched things off that were meant to be kept on, and we've forced things on that were better left off—breaking God's intended design for our work on Monday.

This is the reality of Monday Morning Atheism: the way many of us approach work as if God doesn't exist—essentially switching God off. And for many years it was my approach as well, all because of three little lies that affected my thoughts and behavior. Based on over 5,000 surveys collected during our years of research (see Appendix A), it seems that you and I are not alone. Even those of us that love our jobs are affected.

This book was written to help ordinary people like us experience God as we work. Imagine your workday with peace, power, and purpose. In other words, working God's way, not our way. I am confident that together we can find brighter work days ahead.

Let's get started while there's still plenty of light!

Doug Spada

P.S. Join me now at www.MondaySwitch.com to get your free Switch Quiz Profile showing the spiritual traits unique to your work challenges.

How to Best Use This Book

FOR YOU:

Like a treasure map, this book starts you on an exciting personal journey. You can read a section each week, being sure to use the resources at the end of each section to focus you for the following work week. In particular, practice at least one suggestion or idea for the entire next week. To get the most from this book, be sure to start by accessing the Switch Quiz (www.MondaySwitch.com) which identifies your top spiritual work challenges. This is a lifetime journey, made one work week at a time. If you open your heart and allow God to change the way you work, your coming year at work will be brighter than ever before. Once you finish this book, you can start the powerful six-step video series called The Switch!

FOR GROUPS AND TEAMS:

Taking this journey in the company of others will enhance your experience. This book can be used as a five-week interactive experience for small groups. So grab your coworkers or friends to experience this book with you, and then set a time when you can meet weekly to discuss it. Consider giving this book to each person in your group. More ideas at www.MondaySwitch.com

FOR MINISTRIES, CHURCHES, AND BUSINESS:

As a leader, you have an incredible opportunity— and a responsibility—to help people grow in and through their work lives. Work is where people spend most of their time and experience the majority of their relationships. This book and its companion video series (The Switch) have been developed with leaders like you in mind, as a way to help you better serve your people. Take a bold step and lead your entire organization through this book. You will be amazed at the results! Since it has been designed for both individual and small group use, you can integrate it in numerous ways. It's our prayer that the transformation you see will increase your effectiveness and your daily impact in your community.

Short Circuits

Introduction:
When Wrong Assumptions
Cause Big Problems

August 14, 2003, was a nice hot summer day for millions in the United States. People were trying to keep cool, and air conditioners were humming feverishly trying to keep up. Soon transmission lines carrying the extra electrical load began to overheat. By late afternoon, some lines had become super-hot, softening and stretching under their own weight. One of those lines was drooping near trees that had not been sufficiently trimmed, and at 4:11 p.m., that line touched a branch. Thousands of volts of electricity instantly surged towards the ground. This short circuit was a faulty connection causing currents to increase and leading to big time damage.

The abnormally high power load on that line was immediately rerouted through other paths in the already strained power grid. Quickly overloaded, these lines also tripped their breakers, forcing the surging power to find yet another line. And so it went, one after the other in quick succession—a cascading blackout that swept across the northeastern United States and Canada.

Meanwhile, people in the area were going about their normal routines, just finishing up another day at work—a call center employee in the middle of a phone call, a marketing team gathered in a planning meeting, a construction worker installing a door, a supervisor reading a report in her cubicle, a bank teller completing a transaction...

Then, with a sudden click, their workplaces went black. Instantly, fifty-five million people were working in the dark.

Panicked crowds in Manhattan, New York, fled their offices and flooded the streets. Stoplights were dead, traffic was gridlocked. Mass transit was at a standstill. The city was paralyzed and power would not be fully restored for two days. The lights at work were off in the whole region, and it started with a single short circuit.

Spiritual blackout at work is a similar event, but in many ways even more significant. Life is wired by God to operate in a capacity that depends on Him—things are supposed to flow a certain way. But when we ignore the strongest part of the system—the power plant itself—and work as if God does not exist, we take on a massive load—a burden that we were never intended to carry. As happened on that hot day, we end up with a cascading spiritual blackout that leaves us working as if there is no God at all, we switch OFF, we become Monday Morning Atheists.

In order to switch God back on in our work, we have to fix the bad spiritual wiring—the foolish changes we've made to God's design. This faulty wiring is wrong thinking, the untrue assumptions that are behind the personal short circuits that cause big problems, real pain, and confusing detours.

Our own struggles often go unaddressed because they are usually subtle and hard to detect. This book is a way to find and fix those kinds of problems. It might seem evasive at first, but God has a great interest in you finding His Life in your work. I can relate because God has led me through this same journey of discovery. Actually, I am still on this journey.

You will find truths in this book that will help guide you to a new place at work, a place most of us never knew existed. No more will you have to accept work just draining life from you; you are actually going to find new life in your work! God's life—a life full of incredible power, peace, and purpose—is waiting.

To get started, you first need to take a closer look at how work issues appear in real life for you. This will be an important key to your journey forward. We have designed a unique personal profile tool, the Switch Quiz, that calculates your top spiritual work challenges from among the 30 most prevalent. *If you haven't yet, please stop right now and take five minutes to finish this quiz at www.MondaySwitch.com.*

Now, let's begin this journey by looking into the story of a person who wanted to do right, but was derailed by serious short circuits and a looming blackout. That person would be me, Doug, a recovering Monday Morning Atheist.

Identify Your Key Work Challenges First!

Get the most from this book. Take 5 minutes and receive your free Switch Quiz Profile, revealing character and behavioral traits unique to your work challenges.

Go to www.MondaySwitch.com

Who Turned Out the Lights?

Me, an Atheist?

> "There are pseudo-atheists who think that they believe in God, but who in reality deny his existence by each one of their deeds."
>
> **JACQUES MARITAIN**

My life felt like it was over as I checked into the hotel that first night. It was clear that I couldn't go back to my house, so I'd gone out into the night.

I'll always remember the emptiness I experienced when I finally got to the hotel room. I stepped inside with my bag, and the door swung shut behind me with a loud metallic slam. I was alone in the pitch black, and that darkness was a perfect reflection of my life. I fumbled to find the light switch on the wall, searching desperately for some light.

For years it seemed like I was on top of the world. I was successful by many standards, riding the wave of my ambition and an economic boom, earning more money than I'd ever imagined, and living in a nice house with a wonderful family. But inside, things had been falling apart due to some painful short circuits in my spiritual wiring. I had been living on burnt fumes, always working. My job filled my life all the way to the margins, and I'd left no space on my page. My priorities were messed up. I would have said that I believed in God, but the ugly truth was that I was working and living much like He did not exist at all.

Now here I was, out in the middle of the night, with nowhere to go but a cheap motel. I had a sick feeling as I thought about it all. I had

...all of it dragged down into a hole that I couldn't stop digging...

traded God's promises for the lies of this world, and my family—and my God—were anything but impressed. I had shut God out of my work, and without Him, disaster crept in. My inner character had collapsed beyond repair, and my marriage was sinking rapidly—all of it dragged down into a hole that I couldn't stop digging.

That night at the hotel, surrounded and filled by darkness, I fell beside the bed and wept into the polyester covers. My pride, my success, my sophistication—none of it meant anything to me as all I could think about was the possibility of my marriage and career slipping through my fingers. And slip it did. I was about to lose everything I cared about in the world.

My life was caving in around me; I saw no way out. I was suffocating under my own hidden pain caused by me trying to run my life on my own terms. The truth was that while I had been trying to do the Christian thing here and there, I was missing the main point: true Life. That problem had been masked by my ambition and outward success, letting me deny the growing awareness of the pain and hurt my wife was experiencing as well.

My striving and normal clever coping mechanisms simply would not pull me out of this situation. In many ways, they were what got me there in the first place. So there I was, crying out to God, overwhelmed by it all. The darkness was crushing.

I finally found the light switch on the wall and flipped it. Light pierced the darkness, and I could see. And there, on the nightstand, was a Gideon Bible. And—amazingly—it lay open, as if waiting for me in that hotel room that I had never been to before. As my eyes adjusted to the light, I noticed it was folded open to the book of Isaiah, chapter 43. My eyes fell to the right side of the page, to verses one and two, and I heard my heavenly Father speak directly to my hurting soul.

> **"Don't be afraid, I've redeemed you.**
>> **I've called your name. You're mine.**
>
> **When you're in over your head,**
>> **I'll be there with you.**
>
> **When you're in rough waters,**
>> **you will not go down.**
>
> **When you're between a rock and a hard place,**
>> **it won't be a dead end—**
>
> **Because I am God, your personal God,**
>> **the Holy One of Israel, your Savior."**
>
> **(Isaiah 43:1–2, MSG)**

Right then and there, I knew that a divine purpose was being revealed to me, and I was no longer going to live or work like it all depended on me. I had found the switch, and suddenly the lights started to go on in my soul.

My story of struggling with spiritual darkness at work is not as unique as you may think. Over the last several years, I've been a part of an organization that has studied the realities of people's work lives, surveying over 5,000 individuals like you and me from every walk of life and vocation (see Appendix A). What we found is that many well-meaning Christians are fumbling in the night trying to find their way at work without God. And many of them are zealously working on as if nothing is the matter—blind to the circumstance they are in.

Working in the Dark

What is wrong? How did we find ourselves here? What has led to our derailed work lives? To put it simply, we have left God out of our work, and in doing so, we've switched off His Light as well. That's a big problem, and we need to understand why.

The word "light" is one of the most frequently used words in the Bible, and for good reason. Just as light is needed to get around in the physical world, we require God's Light to move through life spiritually. Without His Life and Light, we have all kinds of trouble getting around—we stumble, we get disoriented, and sometimes we hurt ourselves. We move in a direction that seems right, but we often end up somewhere totally different instead.

How did we find ourselves here?

Without God filling our life at work, it's no wonder why work feels like such an empty experience and why work so often causes real pain for us in life.

The shocking truth is that you and I and many others like us who profess to follow Jesus end up working in spiritual darkness all too often. Why is it that we can turn our backs on God even though rationally we know this is not wise or right?

It might be because we often think about turning away from God in dramatic terms. Something like leaving the church, having an affair, or getting involved with something obviously wrong. In reality, many of us who end up drifting into a kind of spiritual darkness do so in ways that are far more subtle.

PETER
IT Specialist

"I know I shouldn't ignore God at work, but it's so easy to do here."

The demands of life constantly pull against what God wants for us, drawing us away inch by inch. In fact, even things that seem good according to the world can be subtle ways to separate us from what is truly good according to God. Those gradual and seemingly small steps eventually place us much farther away than we ever realized. For many of us, this slow, steady drifting away from God has happened in our work. It's a drift caused by a series of choices and habits that may seem mostly harmless at the time—like stretching the truth about hours on a time sheet, working late while family members' needs go unmet at home, or simply getting so focused on work that we no longer have space in our brain to ponder other important things.

...even things that seem good can separate us from God.

That's why it may be hard for us to admit or even realize that God simply no longer seems relevant to us in the way we work. We have conditioned ourselves to work without God. We work like we are on our own, like it's all depending on us. We have switched

God off at work, choosing to go ahead blindly. In other words, we are Monday Morning Atheists.

Even though most of us who are reading this book probably believe in God, at certain times in our work lives we function just like atheists. None of us are entirely exempt— we all do it on occasion. It's just a question of when and in what area we switch off our spiritual lights at work. Whether the lights have always been off, or they are just starting to dim, the truth is the same—for many of us, we often work as if God does not exist. When we approach our work week without including God, we have to be honest: we are practicing Monday Morning Atheism.

Atheist (noun)
Definition:
Someone who does not believe in God.

Monday Morning Atheist (noun)
Definition:
Someone who believes in God but who works like He does not exist.

Again, this is an observation, not an opinion. We have primary research including surveys of thousands of workers (Appendix A). They have told us a lot. They've told us their struggles—and demonstrated that personal and professional problems stemming from Monday Morning Atheism are significant and widespread.

Our Spiritual Bumps and Bruises

The actual work and character issues facing us today are numerous. As we try to navigate work without God, our souls suffer many bumps and bruises. We often feel like a slave to our schedule as we battle with stress and discouragement. Our spouse may be consumed by his or her career, or maybe we're the one being consumed. There are conflicts surrounding office politics such as gossip, slander, favoritism, and criticism. Some of us have significant discontentment with our paycheck or position. We struggle with anger and the pressure to fudge our ethics, and sometimes we come face-to-face with sexual temptation at work.

...our wayward way of working has cost us...

A big issue today is worry over job insecurity; this is now a way of life for many. But even when the economy is rolling happily along, it never really delivers what it promises. The intoxicating effects of money only mask the underlying pain and great costs our work imposes on the rest of our life. Many of us are addicted to our work. It has consumed us. We are never off. We are always on. And, as I was lamenting in that hotel room, our wayward way of working has cost our marriages and family relationships dearly. Carrying the unending stress of it all has even undermined our health. The rampant illnesses of heart disease, obesity, hypertension, diabetes, and depression are in many cases symptoms of the unbalanced way we have learned to work.

> **"I wish my dad spent more time with me."**

When God's guiding principles are switched off as a force shaping the way we work, we lose our moral compass. Expediency becomes the end-all and be-all. Right and wrong are sacrificed in the name of profit. The price we pay for our godless work lives is the loss of our integrity and wholeness.

My problems almost cost me my marriage, and while most people's issues with work are not as dramatic, they are just as real.

Perhaps your issue is that you are chronically bored at work. Your job is just a job, and you are not sure what its purpose is besides paying the bills. The routine often seems so futile and pointless: go to work, do what is required, and then come home. You live for weekends, holidays, and that week or two of vacation to hopefully enjoy yourself. But beyond that, your job is a big yawn. Maybe this is because work has no higher purpose. You have no sense of life at work. It's no surprise that, according to a national survey of workers, over 55% of us are dissatisfied with our jobs.

...according to a national survey, over 55% of us are dissatisfied with our jobs.

There is another smaller but equally fragile group reading this that deserves special mention: those of us who honestly like our jobs yet fail to include God anyway. Perhaps you are quite happy with what you do. It's work you do well, and you've been rewarded

HELEN
Real Estate Assistant

"I'm around so much conflict...I don't know how to deal with this."

for it. Yet you've fallen into the subtle yet fatal trap of disregarding God during the work day. You may try to be a good person and work hard, but in the end, it simply has nothing to do with God. As a result, in the long run your job or career is a hollow success.

Finding New Life in Work

Given these realities of work, how are we to cope? Walking away is not an option. We need a job to live. We all need to work, and Monday mornings will keep coming. For some of us, there is a natural fit with our job and times are good. For many, the job feels like walking in someone else's shoes. It only leaves blisters on the soul. Some are in even more pain, hanging on for dear life, having lost a job or fearing what may happen soon.

Regardless of how we feel about our work, all of us feel its irritations—there may be some "pebble in your shoe" as you walk into the office or arrive on the job site. It may be the long hours, the money, or the job description. It may be dashed dreams, the looming specter of unemployment, or the people that seem to stand in your way. It may be the irritating boss or the irksome employees or the time away from home. Sometimes it's the haunting question of whether your work has any worth at all. Almost all of us can see evidence of Monday Morning Atheism all around us.

But whatever your situation, I know one thing for certain: Today, right where you are, God wants to bring you hope. He can help you turn the lights back on—showing you a new reason for your work.

God wants to bring you hope.

I speak from experience because God did it for me. He redeemed and restored my family and continues to help me grow out of my old Monday Morning Atheism. He will do the same for you.

We can turn the power back on in our work life, rejecting the pull of the lies that lead to Monday Morning Atheism; and when the lights are back on, we can again move freely. When we stop working as Monday Morning Atheists, we can rediscover purpose in our work. Remember, this is the kind of life promised by God! Jesus even promised, "I have come that they may have life, and that they have it more abundantly" (John 10:10, NKJV). It's a life that leads to joy, fulfillment, and a power that comes from following the desires of a loving God. This pursuit of work full of God's purpose and meaning has changed thousands of lives, and it has the revolutionary power to change yours as well.

...we can rediscover purpose in our work.

Some of you have experienced that wake-up call, like I did that night in the hotel room. Others may be noticing a pull at your heart that is moving you to a new place. Maybe you are seeing some of the spiritual challenges in your own work but don't know where to turn for a solution. Or possibly you're just starting your work career, maybe even still in school, asking, "How can I do this and avoid these mistakes?" You're in the right place.

We are about to explore three false assumptions commonly found in our thinking about work, lies that act like short circuits in our spiritual work lives and cause everything to go dim. The keys to a renewed life at work are found in tackling these lies:

> **"Only some of life is spiritual."**
> **"I'm alone and it's all up to me."**
> **"My work is just a waste."**

Remember, God never made you to work without Him and He never created you to function as a Monday Morning Atheist. You are not designed to stumble through the dark. So go ahead: untangle these hazardous short circuits and switch on the lights!

Work Life Illumination

 "Arise, shine; for your light has come, and the glory of the LORD has risen upon you." Isaiah 60:1 (NASB)

Dear God,

Sometimes I work without even thinking of You. Thank You for wanting to bless my work! Work can be so stressful and even painful at times. Even on good days, I sometimes question if there is any point to it. I really need You at work. I want to work Your way, not mine. God, please change the way I work...

"It is so great knowing God is right here with me.
I can feel peace and confidence as I deal with the stresses,
challenges, and even the opportunities at work."
—Rachel, Executive

Switch Check

☑ □ **Yes** □ **No** Do you frequently dread going to work?

□ **Yes** □ **No** Is work a source of pain for yourself or your family?

□ **Yes** □ **No** Do you worry too much about work?

□ **Yes** □ **No** Do you like or love your work but still yearn for more?

□ **Yes** □ **No** Are you discouraged or unsure work is worth the effort?

If you answered "yes" to any of these, there is a good chance you are affected to some degree by Monday Morning Atheism.

Reflections

1) Do you sometimes work like a Monday Morning Atheist? How?

2) Think about a time when you felt as if you were going to drown in the challenges you faced in your job. What was the situation and how did you respond?

3) Describe how work may be a source of trouble or pain for yourself or your family.

Bright Ideas

- Buy an actual light switch from a hardware store and place it on your desk. Flip the switch throughout the day to remind you of your ON/OFF God choice.

- Confide in someone you trust about the work issues you are thinking about. Ask for their honest opinion and input.

- Draw a light switch on the top of your notepad or "to-do" list every day.

Stop the Switch

A more abundant worklife is on the way. If you haven't already, go to www.MondaySwitch.com and take the 5-minute Switch Quiz. You can find the spiritual behavior traits common to your work challenges.

Notes and Ideas

Spiritual Schizophrenia

Short Circuit:
Only Some of Life is Spiritual

"The worst lies are not the ones we tell, but the ones we live."

ANONYMOUS

Do I have Spiritual Schizophrenia?

John Nash had a stellar career. He was a brilliant thinker, mathematician, and economist; a Nobel Prize winner; universally recognized as brilliant. From the very beginning of his schooling, he seemed destined for greatness. At a very young age, his advisor recommended him to graduate studies at Ivy League schools with a letter of only one sentence: "This man is a genius." At age twenty-two, he had already graduated from Princeton with a doctorate in Mathematics. His dissertation was only twenty-eight pages, but it revolutionized math and economics. His creative intellect was legendary. He taught at Princeton and MIT, two of the most prestigious universities in the world. Truly, John Nash had a career most could only dream of.

But soon, tragedy struck. While at the top of his profession at age thirty, he began to hear voices in his head. These voices led him to believe that he was really a secret agent who was the target of dark, powerful forces in a cold-war communist conspiracy.

He imagined encoded messages in almost everything he read. John Nash had become schizophrenic.

Schizophrenia is the psychological disorder ascribed to a person medically diagnosed as having a split or "disassociation" between the rational and emotional parts of the brain. The word "schizophrenia" comes from the Greek words *schizein*, "to split," and *phrenia* meaning "the mind." People diagnosed with schizophrenia may go through life struggling to navigate two or more apparent realities. At times, they may see the world as it really is, but when under the influence of schizophrenia, their mind and emotions can build a false reality of their own.

Do You Struggle with Spiritual Schizophrenia?

A Monday Morning Atheist is living with a kind of "spiritual schizophrenia," a case of having a split mind with God and work on opposing sides. This spiritual schizophrenia comes from a false belief that life divides neatly into different compartments

ANDY
Automotive Technician

"Sure, I'm a Christian. But what does that have to do with my job?"

...a case of having a split mind with God and work on opposing sides.

with only a small part of life being truly spiritual and the rest being non-spiritual, or at least spiritually neutral.

In this belief, the spiritual aspect of life involves activities like church (when we make it), prayer (when we are in a tight jam), and possibly reading our Bible (if we are really "religious"). Other spiritual activities like serving the homeless or short-term missions may also qualify. But thinking that these types of activities are the only things that really matter to God is a mistake. Today we too often see our job purely as an earthly enterprise, and we rarely see any spiritual component at all. We need to absorb a truth that teacher and author A. W. Tozer once expressed this way: "It is not what a man does that determines whether his work is sacred or secular, but why he does it."

Why do you work? Do you ever treat your work as if it were unrelated to God? If so, then you've probably struggled with spiritual schizophrenia and the dim and lifeless work that comes with it.

Being Blind to the Problem

Many years ago I was on the verge of making a decision that would change the course of my life. During this period I had a conversation with a colleague of mine named Peter. At the time, I was the CEO of a consulting company, but I was feeling like I needed a way to make a more meaningful impact—to be significant in God's eyes.

Peter recognized this, I think, and asked, "So, Doug, how's life?" I answered, "It's okay, but I'm feeling a little unsettled. I've been trying to figure out my mission in life. And right now I know God is calling me to help in a way that matters most to Him—probably something here at church like evangelism, or at least being on staff to help our church's mission."

At that point, he challenged me with a simple and powerful question: "Well, Doug, let me back things up a little. Tell me about your work—what has God been doing in your life Monday to Friday? Who have you been influencing?"

That question almost seemed off-topic at first, irrelevant to the more spiritual aspirations I had in mind. But Peter continued to say, "Doug, I am trying to get at something a little different. Have you ever considered that maybe God has plans for you in the workplace? Ministry plans through your job?"

Even as I answered, I was beginning to understand the problem in my thinking. "Huh. Well, I...I guess I haven't ever thought of my actual 'work' in terms of mission or ministry before."

Looking back, I find it sad, because here I was, a guy spending over fifty hours a week working, and I was seeing it as a spiritual write-off. Regrettably, I was actively looking for a way to contribute to God's kingdom, but I was only thinking in terms of quitting work and following a narrow idea of "God's work." I was totally in the dark about the problem, a victim of a full-blown short circuit in my spiritual wiring that had switched off a huge chunk of my life from God's influence.

Ironically, I was just a step away from joining the staff of my church in some capacity despite my own spiritual confusion. Serving in your church is a great thing, but the tragedy is that somehow, even while taking the question so seriously, I got the idea that my work was not spiritual at all. Looking back, I realize that I was operating with spiritual schizophrenia; as a result, I was thinking like an atheist for most of the week. Since that time, I've found that my story of having a huge spiritual blind spot is not an exception but the norm. Seeing work as inherently non-spiritual is a major false assumption causing Monday Morning Atheism to grow in our work lives.

My Narrow Thinking

When I held up my work in comparison to my ideas about what I thought God wants for us, somehow I came away with the message that my work was not that important. I was trapped by the assumption that only things I did in connection with church or formal ministry could be spiritual. "If I could just go into full-time

"I am so conflicted almost every day."

Christian ministry, I would be happy"—this was my private thinking. Some of you have had this very same thought.

This divided view of life saturates our value system. We think that the big questions about eternity are all that matter to God, that He wants us to think about souls and nothing else. But limiting our idea of what is spiritual in that way attempts to put God in a little box of our own design and He's not meant to be confined to that.

Dorothy Sayers, a famed Christian writer from Oxford, once said it well: "[The church] has allowed work and religion to become separate departments, and is astonished to find that, as a result, the secular work of the world is turned to purely selfish and destructive ends, and that the greater part of the world's intelligent workers have become irreligious, or at least, uninterested in religion."

Working Truth: Everything is His

So we're starting to see this idea, that only some types of work are spiritual is flawed. It denies the biblical truth that everything was created by God for His glory. It fails to see that everything that exists is His domain. Abraham Kuyper, a Christian philosopher and the prime minister of the Netherlands, once said, "In the total expanse of human life there is not a single square inch of which the Christ, who alone is sovereign, does not declare, 'That is mine!'" In reality, everything in creation was made by God and belongs to Him. "For in Him all things were created: things in heaven and on earth, visible and invisible, whether thrones or powers or rulers or authorities; all things have been created through Him and for Him" (Colossians 1:16 NIV). Everything in the world, everything in your life—it's all His.

> **Everything in the world is His.**

The Apostle Paul wrote to Christians living in the pagan city of Corinth, "Whatever you do, do it all for the glory of God" (I Corinthians 10:21, NIV). He wanted them to make sure that there was no division in their lives between their relationship with God and what they did on a daily basis. God created all of life, so therefore, all of life is spiritual. We are on a divine mission for God while at work.

Whatever your specific work situation, believing that God is not interested in the work that takes up so much of your time will lead to a schizophrenic spiritual life. We become spiritually deadened to most of what we do during our waking hours, and soon enough the lights dim and leave us in the dark spiritually. We can't let that happen. We spend more time working than we do in any other activity—more than home responsibilities and certainly more than church. We have left our faith out of work as if it did not matter, and everything about work has suffered for it. Your heavenly Father wants to be Lord of everything. Everything is His, and acknowledging that fact is part of what we were designed to do.

We spend more time working than we do in any other activity…

ANNE
Marketing Consultant

"I find myself being two-faced at work like everyone else, and I can't seem to stop."

Think About God's Reputation

This false notion about what is and isn't spiritual causes us to live hypocritically as well. In fact, this is the number one reason most people give for unbelief—the hypocrisy of Christians they work with or live around. On Sunday we see the world through a spiritual lens, but when we get ready to work on Monday, our behavior all too often can't be distinguished from anyone else's. We claim to have seen the light, but many of us stumble around in the darkness the entire time our coworkers see us at work. This contradiction has done immeasurable harm to the reputation of God's character and love.

"Lack of loyalty and honesty at my work is a huge challenge for me."

Of course, this particular area of wrong thinking goes well beyond the boundaries of our work. Studies show that, on almost every measure, nominal Christians are just as likely to lie, cheat, and get divorced as the general population.

Working (and living) Monday to Friday as if there was no God of Sunday results in a two-faced way of living. This smears God's reputation particularly among those we work with. What are we to do?

Living a Bold and Flavorful Life

This attempt to separate life into the spiritual and the non-spiritual is similar to the way a frozen dinner's little white tray is divided up into different compartments, each part tightly sealed by cellophane into separate spaces. With these meals, the manufacturer doesn't want these various parts to spill over into one another. To keep it neat and clean, they compartmentalize everything. If this sounds bland and sterile, you're right. It's food built for convenience, not for quality.

Similarly, we are tempted to limit faith to a small area of life for the sake of extra convenience. We often compartmentalize our lives, keeping God separate from areas such as our finances, sex life, and work so that everything is safe, separated, and easy.

The result, of course, is unappetizing. To gain convenience, quality is sacrificed. And to those on the outside looking in, it probably looks about as good as a frozen dinner.

On the other hand, consider a stir-fry—bold and flavorful. Stir-fry is very different from a frozen dinner's careful separation—the opposite, in fact. In a stir-fry dinner, all the ingredients are

God never intended any part of life to be kept apart from a relationship with Him.

sautéed in the same sauce along with spices and high heat. You toss everything around violently, mixing it up thoroughly so that everything gets covered in the good sauce. That's what gives it flavor. Living with God is meant to be bold and delicious, like a stir-fry, spiritually flavoring every aspect of life. It was never meant to be a frozen dinner of cellophane, cardboard, and unappetizing fare. God never intended any part of life to be kept apart from a relationship with Him. He is the ingredient who should touch all of our thoughts and actions.

Fixing this short circuit—the one that tells us that work is not spiritual and is separate from God—makes us more likely to stay switched ON in our work. Is it any wonder that work can be a bland, lifeless effort when we keep God separate from it? It's only when we address this problematic thinking that work begins to take in the sense of life and purpose that comes from God. Just by knowing this truth about your work, it can seem immediately brighter. Remember, God wants to be included in all of life, and where He is invited, life and purpose are sure to follow.

Work Life Illumination

 "Then Jesus again spoke to them, saying, 'I am the Light of the world; he who follows Me will not walk in the darkness, but will have the Light of life.'" John 8:12 (NASB)

Dear God,

I am finally realizing that You are interested in my work. Thank You for walking with me no matter what I am doing. Help me as I face the challenges of today. I need Your guidance and direction. Grow me spiritually through my work. Thank You for Your care and love...

"I am starting to feel whole again knowing
God never leaves me, even at work. I am seeing places
where I was headed in the wrong direction."
—David, Engineer

Switch Check

☑   □ **Yes** □ **No**   Do I behave one way at work and another way at home or church?

□ **Yes** □ **No**   Do I rarely think about God at work?

□ **Yes** □ **No**   Do I think work is cursed, mostly bad, or worldly?

□ **Yes** □ **No**   Do I think pastors or missionaries are more blessed than I am?

□ **Yes** □ **No**   Do I feel my work does not matter to God and has little spiritual value?

If you answered "yes" to any of these, there is a good chance that you are struggling to some degree with spiritual schizophrenia.

Reflections

1) When was the last time you saw something at work that was contrary to your values or religious beliefs? What was it?

2) Give an example of a behavior or attitude in you that is different at work than when you're at home or church.

3) How would you work differently if you knew that Jesus would be your customer or your coworker?

Bright Ideas

- Keep a packet of soy sauce in your desk drawer or briefcase to remind you that God is the sauce that flavors all you do.

- If you do something wrong at work, admit it. Keeping short accounts is healthy for relationships.

- Go out of your way every day to do something extra for someone. When you catch someone else doing well at work, tell them you noticed.

Stop the Switch

Let's switch on the lights. Use the 5-minute Switch Quiz to pinpoint your most prevalent spiritual challenges at work. Get it free at www.MondaySwitch.com.

Notes and Ideas

The Absent God

Short Circuit:
I'm Alone and It's All Up to Me

"Surely the Lord is in this place, and I was not aware of it."

JACOB

Jacob was a self-made man, a titan of the agriculture industry with great wealth and power. But his empire was a fragile one. Because he was dependent on the health of his livestock, the prosperity of his business was constantly at the mercy of the climate and disease from one year to the next. Drought and disease were always lurking threats. If that wasn't enough, even once he had scratched and clawed his way to the top, he had to watch his back—his own uncle kept trying to rip him off.

Perhaps, then, it's not surprising that Jacob often felt that it was him against the world—that he had to look out for himself. He felt like he had to fight to get ahead. Jacob's reliance on himself had helped him get the upper hand throughout his life, so he was determined to continue to take care of his own interests.

But this approach didn't always cause Jacob to make the best choices. While his intense drive played a role in his success, it had also caused him to lose sight of his own personal values. On one occasion, blatantly so. With more wealth at stake, he manipulated his brother into renouncing his share of the family business; Jacob was willing to cast his brother aside in service of himself and his self-centered ambition.

For his entire career, whether fighting the weather, fending off threats, or fighting his own family, Jacob had always been engaged in a lonely struggle. He assumed there would always be winners and, as a result, losers. By using his own intellect and desire, he always managed to come out ahead of others.

It's a familiar story, the same kind we've seen in movies and heard in the news: the rising person at work doing exactly what he wants with little concern or need for others. Many of these stories end with a disaster or a scandal, but one night, Jacob's story took an amazing turn.

The big change in Jacob's life came abruptly and without warning. Late one night he suddenly found himself wrestling with someone incredibly powerful. Jacob was normally a self-confident man who could only imagine himself winning, but now he was completely overpowered. He was helpless. He was defeated. He had lost.

But when it was over, Jacob had a powerful realization. This was a spiritual experience. He knew, without any uncertainty, that what he experienced was actually a battle with God over his heart and soul. For the first time, Jacob had met an opponent he couldn't conquer, and he was humbled. In his quest for success, he had been ignoring God completely, and God had stepped in as a reminder of His authority. After this incident, Jacob said, "Surely the Lord is in this place, and I was not aware of it." For Jacob, it was a place in the desert. For me, it was a cheap hotel room. Where have you wrestled? Does it really have to be a struggle, or can we learn from Jacob and others?

Where have you wrestled?

RODNEY
Shipping Supervisor

"I can't trust these people; if I don't do it, it won't get done."

Jacob's story gives us an example of a person discovering yet another of the three short circuits that lead to Monday Morning Atheism: "I'm alone and it's all up to me." He thought that his work was constantly being undermined by others and that others were the enemy, but the real problem was the darkness caused by his own thinking. My story at the beginning of this book developed from the same roots, the same ones that so many struggle with.

What Can We Learn from Jacob?

It's highly possible that you have read about Jacob before or at least heard his story. If so, you probably recognized he's the Jacob of the Bible whose story in Genesis was given to us by God to help us understand the need for an active relationship with Him—how we can't afford to switch Him off. Clearly, the struggles we're dealing with today are old ones, and they're problems God thought were important enough to record for us to study all these years later.

The sense that God is absent—and the associated belief that it all depends on us as individuals—generates this particular error in our thinking about work. We have a false assumption about the God we desire to serve, a delusion that He is not with us in our work.

...a delusion that He is not with us in our work.

Once this lie grabs you, it begins to stretch out in other parts of your thinking. It says that He does not really matter to your job. It says that God is irrelevant or absent. And since He is absent, that means that you're left to your own resources to solve problems at work by yourself. You have to fix it, and you're the only one who will solve it. Of course, this inner conviction of forced self-reliance is contrary to God's design for your life. With these thoughts, the lights for your work will begin to flicker and burn out. If you think that God is absent in your work, you will not see God's mission for you in your work. You won't think of His power to help you, and you won't think of His expectation for you to serve Him.

Thankfully, God was gracious and gave us a colorful view of self-reliance in the Bible. A modern paraphrase of Scripture, The Message, really describes this well:

It is obvious what kind of life develops out of trying to get your own way all the time:...a stinking accumulation of mental and emotional garbage; frenzied and joyless grabs for happiness;...paranoid loneliness; cutthroat competition; all-consuming-yet-never-satisfied wants; a brutal temper; an impotence to love or be loved; divided homes and divided lives; small-minded and lopsided pursuits; the vicious habit of depersonalizing everyone into a rival; uncontrolled and uncontrollable addictions; ugly parodies of community. I could go on...

But what happens when we live God's way? He brings gifts into our lives, much the same way that fruit appears in an orchard—things like affection for others, exuberance about life, serenity. We develop a willingness to stick with things, a sense of compassion in the heart, and a conviction that a basic holiness permeates things and people. We find ourselves involved in loyal commitments, not needing to force our way in life, able to marshal and direct our energies wisely. (Galatians 5:19–23)

Wow, what a contrast! God's truth shows us that relying only on

So why do we keep trying to do it all?

our own results is a deadened existence. But reliance on God and His Son Jesus can bring true life to work. We simply can't do it alone.

So why do we keep trying to do it all? That question is the key to understanding this particular short circuit.

Knowing What We Are Not

I wish I could tell you I've mastered this problem, but the truth is that I sincerely struggle like many of you. I've had to learn the hard way, and I want to share a perfect example from my own work life.

Many years ago, I had the opportunity of running an energy consulting company. I enjoyed great success but learned reliance on God the hard way. Once when I was negotiating an agreement with another company, I sensed God instructing me to avoid these people. He guided me to turn away. He did this through counsel from advisors, verses from the Bible, and the Holy Spirit speaking

to me, along with clear roadblocks that I should have heeded.
What did I do? I gave God a spiritual head nod and went forward.
I thought I could make it work if I was just clever enough. Relying
on myself and my own thinking, just three months later I was in
turmoil and money was being stolen from our firm. In the end, my
insistence on control resulted in our company losing almost
a million dollars.

That is why when we fail to depend on God's help we often end
up frustrated and alone. His plans will come to pass, and if we're
not aligned with His will, we are destined to be frustrated.

It's what I was dealing with, what Jacob was doing, and it's what
many of us are demonstrating when we only consider ourselves
and forget that God is also present and has a perfect plan of His
own. One that doesn't always fit with what we want. I may wish I
could just speak and make the universe turn on a dime, but I can't.
And I doubt you can either. But God can.

It's obvious that we don't have the power or insight that an eternal

It's contrary to the way we've been designed…

God does. As humans, we are all limited and fragile beings—none of us can fathom the amazing power of our Lord. That's why attempting to do everything we want—while ignoring the help and counsel of others—is such a disastrous short circuit. It's contrary to the way we've been designed and the way God wants us to work today. What are we thinking?

Practicing a Critical Truth: "I Am"

Often we fail to remember the most basic aspect of our faith: God is really here. That means He is also there with you when you work. It's the first idea of the Bible, the fact that God is and always has been present: "In the beginning, God…"

God is. It's a truth so essential to our ability to understand God that it's the name He gave Himself: Yahweh, which means "I am." This means that the God who loves you so much is all-powerful, all-knowing, and in every place at the same time. Amazing! He

NATALIE
Lab Technician

"It's so easy to turn God off at work— like He's not even here with me."

...do you work as if He is in you?...

never wanted us to forget that, saying, "This is my name forever, the name by which I am to be remembered from generation to generation" (Exodus 3:14–15, NIV).

Do you work as if "I Am" is with you and partnering with you, or do you work as if He is only present on occasion? Even more, do you work as if He is in you and changing you to make you more like Him?

Please receive this truth: you are never, ever alone. God exists, and He is with you. Until we realize that God is with us when we are working, we will not be freed from Monday Morning Atheism. Until then, we will always struggle to have meaning and life in our work.

Jacob is not the only famous person from the Bible that learned this lesson. David, the slayer of Goliath and among the most famous kings of Israel, reflects on the question of whether God is actually present. He shares this with us in one of his psalms collected in the Bible:

You are familiar with all my ways...Where can I go from your Spirit? Where can I flee from your presence? If I go up to the heavens, you are there; if I make my bed in the depths, you are there...If I settle on the far side of the sea, even there your hand will guide me, your right hand will hold me fast. (Psalm 139:3, 7–10, NIV)

God is present literally everywhere. The heavens and seas seem like natural places for God. Can we apply this idea to our work today? Absolutely. Listen to King David's words in the Bible adapted for our present-day work:

"When I am on the road traveling all week, I feel really isolated."

God, is there anywhere on the job that I can go where you are not already present? Anything I do that you don't care about and watch over? If I work on the top floor of our corporate skyscraper, you're there! If I am a janitor in the basement, you're there! If I am a salesperson flying across the country on a business trip, you are with me.

Wow! Just think of that! Whether you know it or not, God is closely connected with your work. He cares about the challenges you face and the trials you are going through. No matter what you may face or where you may go, He is there with you, and furthermore, he's right in the middle of it. We find out in another promise that He's not only there, He's also ready to help you. He is "an ever-present help in trouble" (Psalm 46:1, NIV).

God is…an ever-present help in trouble.

Do you live in God's presence at work? When we work as if He is not there, as if it is all up to us, we are ignoring these powerful realities and risking a massive blackout in our work life.

In closing, a famous Puritan, Cotton Mather, once wrote: "Oh, let every Christian walk with God when he works at his calling, and act in his occupation with an eye to God." Rather than accept the broken work that excludes God, let's continue pursuing the goal of adding God back into our job descriptions with renewed commitment to remembering His words "I Am." When we add this

to the practical truth we learned in the previous section—
that everything (including work) is spiritual because it belongs
to God and is under His ownership—we are well on our way to
a complete picture of how our work can be given renewed
meaning and joy.

Work Life Illumination

 "At one time you were in the dark. But now you are in the light because of what the Lord has done. Live like children of the light." Ephesians 5:8 (NIRV)

Dear God,

I should have realized it. You have always been here with me at work! So many things feel so out of control or confusing at work and yet I haven't been asking for Your help. I am asking now. Help me pay attention to You every day. I need Your help to do a good job. Please guide me and give me Your strength this week...

"God is really with me at work and I am so grateful
to not feel so alone anymore. He cheers me on and shows me
that I make a difference. I believe there's an awakening
happening in my life like never before."
—Cassandra, RN

Switch Check

☐ **Yes** ☐ **No** Do you frequently struggle to stay in control at work, feeling as if it all depends on you?

☐ **Yes** ☐ **No** Do you sometimes feel isolated or feel like no one cares or appreciates what you do at work?

☐ **Yes** ☐ **No** Do you frequently feel overwhelmed in your work?

☐ **Yes** ☐ **No** Do you feel like you have to fix everyone at work?

☐ **Yes** ☐ **No** Are you fiercely competitive at work rather than looking for ways to help everyone win?

If you answered "yes" to any of these, you could be influenced by the belief that God is absent and that you are alone in your work.

Reflections

1) Do you regularly experience God's presence at work? If so, in what situations? If not, why do you think you don't?

2) What upcoming event at work is tempting you to rely too much on yourself? How can you deliberately rely on God instead?

3) List your last two significant decisions at work. What involvement did God have in them?

Bright Ideas

- Write "God is here" on a Post-it note and put it on your computer monitor.

- On your next work day, pause for one minute before each decision and say, "God, You are with me—let's do this together."

- If you have a desk or bookshelf at work, place a Bible as the first book on your shelf to remind you "God first."

Stop the Switch

God is with you at work. To experience this more fully, take the 5-minute Switch Quiz and pinpoint your most common spiritual work challenges. It's free at www.MondaySwitch.com.

Notes and Ideas

It's Just a Paycheck for Me

Short Circuit:
My Work is Just a Waste

> "Finding satisfaction in all your work—it is a gift from God."
>
> **SOLOMON**

The following stories that open this section aren't about famous scientists or people from the Bible. That's because the third and final short circuit is most plainly seen in the lives of people like you and me. Each of these people struggles with the same problem: the feeling that his or her work is possibly a waste.

Consider Susan, a talented and dedicated employee, who had worked all weekend to have a report ready for presentation to the senior vice president. She canceled commitments to family and friends just to pull it off. After staying up all night to get it done by Monday morning, she showed up only to find out that plans had changed. This was not the first time she had watched hours of work get thrown into the trash can. Physically and emotionally spent, a rising sense of futility came flooding in. She asked herself, "What purpose can my job serve when so much of it seems so useless?"

Then there's John, a man in his fifties, who's reached the top of the ladder in his career field, but now he looks around and realizes that his marriage is falling apart. Coming home late after another long day, he finds his wife is already in bed, and feels

"I have worked so hard for so many years and now things just seem empty. I'm afraid I've been wasting my life."

like a stranger in his own home. After a few minutes of flipping channels on the TV fails to turn up anything to fill his emptiness, he stares out the den window at the darkness and questions the point of it all. For so long he worked to get ahead. He got there, but it's nothing like he thought it would be. Now he doesn't know what's left to work for.

Carol is a mom staying home to raise her kids. She reaches the end of each day tired and worn down. She believes in the value of shaping the lives of her young children, but the routine of a homemaker often leaves her feeling unchallenged. She privately wonders if she would be personally more fulfilled using her skills in a career of her own. But for Carol, as either a mom or a career woman, she would be short-changing someone.

Joann understands the feeling. She is a single parent working long hours. The treadmill of just trying to make ends meet seems to never end. The hardest part is that she wonders if she is missing her kids' lives in the process. It seems like a "catch-22." Is there some rhyme or reason to the unending rat race?

> **"I clean houses all day. It feels so repetitious. What's the point?"**

Curt is yet another example of a professional in his thirties who has finally seen his dream succeed, but now finds he does not have the time to enjoy the toys that he worked so hard to afford. He wonders if all the sacrifice his career demands is worth the cost. What does he do when his original purpose doesn't have the appeal it first did?

Jason, a new follower of Christ, is not exempt from this dilemma either. He believes there is more to life. Only three years ago, he came to trust Jesus Christ as his friend and savior, but the problem now is that his new sense of purpose has left his daily

KEN
Executive Manager

"Am I really making a difference? I don't feel like what I do counts or that I'm doing anything for God."

work without meaning. He's somehow come to believe that life in this world is not the point, that only eternal life in Jesus is what counts. But he still has to go to work Monday morning to do a job that, from his perspective, is pointless. Is it all a spiritual waste?

So What's the Point?

Questioning the point of our jobs is a gut-check none of us can avoid. The "Why?" question is the great equalizer. It inevitably stops all of us in our tracks, and it will not accept a cliché for an answer. It is, in fact, a question to us from God. We can try to ignore it. We can feed it temporary fixes. We can bribe ourselves with

Does what I do count for something?

our paycheck. We can even be distracted momentarily from the problem with the false hope of greener pastures. Yet, under the surface, it remains unresolved and keeps bubbling back up within us. The questions are unavoidable: Why in the world am I doing this? Does what I do count for something? Is it worth all the trouble? What is the point of my work? What difference will it really make in the end?

"My job just pays the bills…"

We spend most of our waking hours working, but the purpose and meaning of the actual work we do from Monday to Friday often eludes us. What's the point of life if such a major area of it is pointless?

At one time or another, the "Why?" question haunts us, making no exceptions—not even for people doing work that seems interesting or important. Every one of us wonders about the true value of our work, and tragically, for many, it tends to be a question without a satisfying answer.

In the end, we may believe that most of what we do does not matter, and it's this thinking that creates the third short circuit of Monday Morning Atheism: the false belief that our work is just a waste. God thinks differently.

He made work, and He made it matter. When we act like work does not matter, we are acting against God's will. The questions of life become almost impossible if we're searching for the answers in darkness. Without being able to see with the light God provides for us, we are left with a very real sense of uselessness. Sure, we work to pay the bills, but is that all there is? Is that the only point to all the long hours, blood, sweat, and tears we invest in our jobs? Of course not, but when our spiritual wiring is crossed and the lights go out, it becomes hard to see through the pitch black to a life of meaning and purpose that God has waiting for us.

Working In His Image

God's view of work is so important that He headlined it in the very first chapter of the Bible. God originally made work to be experienced in the context of a moment-by-moment intimate relationship with Him. From the very beginning, the Bible paints a picture of our spiritual bond with God in the Garden of Eden as a working relationship.

We already talked about how the Bible begins with the fact of "God's" omnipresence—that He exists and is present everywhere. But Genesis 1:1 tells us something very specific about God. It tells us that God is a creator, a worker. It says, "In the beginning God created the heavens and the earth." God's first act that we know of in the Bible was an act of work. And it was a work that God said was "very good." Work is good because it comes from the very character of who God is. He is a worker.

God created work. It was His idea. Genesis explains how God made even the very place where Adam and Eve were to work, the Garden of Eden. Not only that, but it explains that when God made human beings, He made them in His own likeness with this same capacity to do good work. Work was part of His plan before sin entered the world. He personally designed and commissioned a job just for them:

> Then God said, "Let us make man in our image, in our likeness, and let them rule over the fish of the sea and the birds of the air, over the livestock, over all the earth, and over all the creatures that move along the ground." So God created man in his own image, in the image of God he created him; male and female he created them...God saw all that he had made, and it was very good. (Genesis 1:26-28, 31 NIV)

The opening of the Bible teaches that God's relationship with the first man and woman was a relationship forged at work, pursued at work, and enjoyed at work.

Furthermore, God said in verse 31 that work is "very good," not a necessary evil but actually a part of His perfect plan for creation. We were made for work. Our work has value because He values it.

Can Being a Carpenter Count?

How can we be sure that God values the activities of our jobs and not just the activities we do solely for our faith, what we often see as our spiritual life?

Our work has value because He values it.

Here is a reassuring fact: Jesus was a simple carpenter. He worked almost His entire life on earth at a very low-key job; all but two or three years of His adult life were spent doing manual labor. He must have performed great work because He had a reputation that spread throughout the land: Jesus, the carpenter from Nazareth.

As we look at the life of Jesus, we get a glimpse of how God values us when we spend our time working, even in simple jobs. When Jesus, as a carpenter, came to be baptized, what did His heavenly Father say about Him? "This is My beloved Son, in whom I am well pleased" (Matthew 3:17, NASB).

Jesus had just spent thirty years of His life working with wood and stone, and God said that He was pleased. Wow! Think about that. Jesus was obedient and served through His work, and in the process He pleased God!

Christ fulfilled His ultimate purpose on the cross, but His work on the carpenter's bench in Nazareth had spiritual significance, too. He showed us how to make work count.

Are those of us who, like Jesus, spend years in "secular" work somehow second class in His eyes? The Biblical answer to both questions is emphatically NO. Your work is significant to God!

But My Job Isn't Anything Important to God!

The reason that being a carpenter counts is the same reason your job counts: because no job is too plain or worldly to matter to God when it's done for His glory. The motivation behind the work is what makes it important no matter how common or man-made the task. When the lights are on spiritually, we're able to find the greater purpose and intention in all of work.

When Paul wrote to the Christians in a city called Ephesus, he addressed the issue of how the people worked. Specifically, he spoke to the house slaves, the bottom rung of the Roman world's workforce. These workers did everything that nobody else was willing to do—often filthy and demeaning chores. Paul says something very surprising about these third-rate jobs in his letter: "Serve wholeheartedly, as if you were serving the Lord, not men, because you know that the Lord will reward everyone for whatever good he does, whether he is slave or free" (Ephesians 6:7-8, NIV).

Serve wholeheartedly, as if you were serving the Lord...

In other words, if slaves doing the worst work in the city could work as if they were working for God, making their daily tasks

Know that the Lord will reward everyone for whatever good he does...

acts of service to God, then He would still reward them for having done good work. That's exciting to me. We can have confidence, no matter what we do, that God is satisfied with our work that's done for His glory. So no matter how lofty the job, no matter how lowly the task, God's eyes find value in our work when we do it for Him. It creates a light shining brightly in our work. Whatever you do, if you do it for God, it's worthwhile. It's that simple!

Part of God's Grand Design

As most of us have already experienced, an improper view of our work can ultimately lead to a feeling of discouragement. Without taking God into account, we see much of our time and effort ending up in the trash can. There are the failures, the time lost, and the futile efforts as well as long roads that turn out to be dead ends.

ANDREA
Nurse Case Manager

"I have never thought of my work as important until now."

"I am so frustrated with my job! God, please help me!"

From our limited perspective, it's hard to imagine how some of our failures might actually be put to use by God for a greater purpose. But that's exactly what He does with even our clumsiest efforts to glorify Him.

Remember, God is not bound by time, and His purposes are beyond our understanding. Work that may seem futile from a human perspective can have purpose through His mysterious ways even though they are hard for us to see. When God makes His plans, all of eternity is visible before Him. It may take months, years, or even centuries for his purposes to be fully revealed. Even those people who directly help along the way might not be able to understand what God is up to. But we can hold Paul's promise to the Ephesians as our own: no work done for God is ever a waste.

It's important for us to remember that work is part of the journey in life—an important tool God uses in shaping us as individuals.

It's not just an objective to be accomplished; what we learn through our work experience has eternal significance for our character and spiritual life.

Do Legos Matter to God?

Sometimes the lies we believe can be hard to shake, especially deeply emotional ones involving our value or worth. In working to rewire your soul on this core work belief, it may help to remember that God is the perfect and loving Father, and we are His kids. Maybe you daily need to hear the same affirmation Jesus heard that day He was baptized: that your heavenly Father is pleased with you, that you matter, and that your work matters to Him. A beautiful story from David, the co-author of this book, illustrates this idea well.

When David's son was still young, he often came to him with his latest Lego creation, saying, "Dad, look at what I made! Do you like it, Dad? Is it good?"

Of course, David would say, "Yes, it's great! I love it!" I think we all ask the same question of God about our work at times. Is what I do good? Does it really matter? Is it more than just a paycheck?

Dad, Look at what I made! Do you like it?"

David could have said to his son what many of us often tell ourselves about our own work: "No, son. It's not good because it doesn't have any spiritual value. Your Lego creations have little spiritual use."

But of course that's not what David told his son. He appreciated the work his son had done. It had value even if it lasted but a minute before going back into the Lego box. It was a reflection of his son's creativity and his God-given gifts.

If David, a human father, can see the value in the work of his children, how much more so is the perfect and eternal Father able to appreciate the efforts of His children? We need to really believe that even our "Lego creations"—the things we make that may seem so frivolous and temporary—matter to God too. He appreciates and loves us and takes pleasure in our daily work when it's done for His glory.

Try this. Think about the worth of your job—then imagine yourself as a child again, holding up your handiwork to your heavenly Dad, asking, "Is it good, Daddy? Do you like it?"

Then allow yourself to feel His eternal affirmation and favor. "It reflects My glory, child. That is why I created you. It is very good."

Your work is so much more than just a paycheck!

Work Life Illumination

 "Let your light shine before men in such a way that they may see your good works, and glorify your Father who is in heaven." Matthew 5:16 (NASB)

Dear God,

It amazes me, Lord, that no matter how small or insignificant my work might seem to me...You think that it has value! You not only appreciate my work, but I see that You want to use it to serve others. Teach me to work Your way so I will sense Your presence in my life...

"It is such a relief to no longer carry the load of work by myself anymore. I am actually sleeping better and my co-workers have even noticed my happier attitude lately. I am also getting more done at work and feeling much less pressure."
—Joann, IT Service

Switch Check

 My work feels pointless when...(mark the choices that apply to you)

————— it ends in failure.

————— all I get is grief.

————— I feel I am on a hamster wheel.

————— no one cares.

————— it really doesn't seem to pay in the end.

If you marked one or more of these, you may be struggling with the belief that work is just a waste.

Reflections

1) Think about how your work has made you stronger. Share three ways in which you have grown over the last year.

2) How do you think Jesus saw His work as a carpenter in Nazareth? What did God think about Jesus' work? Does this change your view about what you do every day?

3) What is your "Lego Creation" that you want to hold up for God to see?

Bright Ideas

- Keep a Lego block on your desk or in your pocket to remind you that God likes what you do.

- Make a list of three reasons work is a blessing to you or your family on the back of a pay stub.

- Make a list of the people you benefited this week, directly and indirectly, with the result of your work.

Stop the Switch

Your work has amazing value! Using the 5-minute Switch Quiz to pinpoint behavior traits associated with your work challenges is a critical step. Get it free at www.MondaySwitch.com.

Notes and Ideas

Turning on the Lights

Restoring the Power

> "For the kingdom of God is not in word but in power."
>
> **APOSTLE PAUL**

Up to this point, we've looked at how the three lies of Monday Morning Atheism cause big problems on the job, problems that can be painful and destructive to everything we care about. We've also explored the corresponding truth that fights against each of these lies. For each of the three false assumptions connected to Monday Morning Atheism, we've looked at God's promises that expose the emptiness of those beliefs and behaviors.

I am sure that, for some of you, it may seem that the lights are very dim in certain areas of your work. I know because I still have areas of dimness that I struggle with. This is a process; what is important is that we keep growing. I firmly believe that our work can change for the better—the environment and requirements of our work may not change, but how it affects us and how we engage in it can be totally different.

You can be certain that God is waiting to help you repair any faulty wiring, mend broken circuits, and bring the power back on in your work. He truly desires for you to experience the joy of working with Him daily as a coworker and a friend. This is His nature as a Father and as a provider.

Our next step in this journey is an exciting one: it's time to start putting the ideas we've discussed into action as we take these truths and translate them into real change on the job.

First Things First: Make Sure It's Plugged In...

We've all done it at least once. You're trying to get some piece of machinery to work, maybe an appliance in your home. You've tried everything a dozen times, and it's about time to take it back to the store. Then someone asks sheepishly, "Did you plug it in?"

Did you plug it in?

We can do all the work in the world repairing the short circuits of our beliefs, making sure that we've patched over lies with truth, but if we're not plugged into the ultimate power source, the lights won't stay on.

Real change in our life begins when we plug in to God—specifically, the Holy Spirit, who is our source of strength.

Without that connection, we are essentially powerless, destined to work in the dark. The Holy Spirit is the power grid—the true and abundant source of power needed for running things in our life, for making changes to our character, and for keeping the lights on in our work life. "But you will receive power when the Holy Spirit comes upon you; and you will be my witnesses in Jerusalem, and in Judea and Samaria and to the ends of the earth" (Acts 1:8).

So as you work through this section, make sure that you are plugged in. Begin with a prayer. Open your heart to God and ask for the Holy Spirit to fill you and empower you as you seek to make these changes to your work life. Forgetting to plug in the toaster or appliance can be awkward; but in this case, it's much more critical to be connected to God, the ultimate power source.

Memorizing Truth, Recognizing Falsehood

When you were learning your multiplication tables as a child, did you only read through them once and suddenly know how to do multiplication? Of course not! You had to practice them, going over

RANDALL
Data Analyst

"I see Monday morning totally different. I know God cares about me and my work."

them dozens and dozens of times in order for it to sink in. Only then could you call on them quickly and produce the correct answer.

It's easy to read over something that teaches us a new truth only to have it vanish from our heads and hearts as soon as we step out into the real world. That's a big part of the problem of Monday Morning Atheism in the first place, isn't it? There are some things that are just too easy for us to forget when our week really gets going. So we have to fight against this tendency to switch off if we want to see growth in our work lives.

We need to be able to quickly recognize the lies of Monday Morning Atheism and counteract them just as quickly with God's promises. The more we practice these truths, the easier it will become to remember them. So, let's review some right now.

Following are the three short circuits of Monday Morning Atheism and the scriptural truths that illuminate them. Write them down and commit them to memory this week.

1) **Lie: "Only some of life is spiritual."**

   The Monday Morning Atheist buys into the false idea that work isn't a spiritual activity. This leads us to think that work and God have nothing to do with each other.

   Truth: It all belongs to God. You are a manager of His creation. When you dismiss your work as something non-spiritual, you are forgetting that God is the Lord over everything, including work. In fact, God tells you how to work: "Whatever you do, work at it with all your heart, as working for the Lord" (Colossians 3:23–24, NIV).

2) **Lie: "I am on my own—got to do it myself."**

   Monday Morning Atheism accepts the lie that God is distant or maybe even absent altogether. We operate with a self-sufficient, got-to-do-it-myself attitude.

   Truth: God promises that you are never alone and that He will work through you. We know that God will not abandon us, no matter how high or how low we feel, no matter how hard things get, and no matter how self-sufficient we think we are. He is always there for us, with us, and ready to work through us. "Never will I leave you; never will I forsake you" (Hebrews 13:5, NIV).

3) Lie: "My work is just a waste."

As Monday Morning Atheists, we believe that the tasks in our daily work may be worthless in the eyes of God. We think that our jobs are too small or too pointless or otherwise too empty to be meaningful.

Truth: God delights in what we do. He designed us uniquely, and He enjoys our work like a father delights in a child. If a human father feels delight in the work of his children, no matter how simple, then imagine how much more God, the perfect Father, delights in our work. While we may often feel that our work is unimportant, He delights in our efforts as a reflection of His glory in creation. "Whatever you do, do it all for the glory of God" (I Corinthians 10:31, NIV).

When we lose sight of these basic truths, we can get off track without even realizing it. Remember to commit these truths to memory. If you can spot a short circuit forming and fix it with truth, God's light will continue to shine in your work.

Practice Makes Progress

The saying is "practice makes perfect," and while it's unrealistic to expect that we'll become perfect any time soon, with practice we can certainly make some great progress.

Now that you've been introduced to the truths of Monday Morning Atheism, you may already have some ideas on how to practice better habits in your work life. We've also included additional ideas at the end of each previous section, and for a whole suite of personal studies, resources and tools visit www.MondaySwitch.com.

Knowing what's wrong is not the same thing as fixing it. We all have areas in our lives that need addressing but we ignore

JANINE
Accountant

"My entire perspective and the way I experience work has completely changed!"

anyway. To make a real change, we have to commit to taking action, one step at a time.

Knowing what is wrong is not the same thing as fixing it.

Below, we have documented a list of action ideas just to get you started. Pick two of the practices and commit to doing them each day for the next fifteen work days. We are building habits here. Even one good practice done daily for fifteen work days will provide surprising results.

Of course, that is only if you have the power of the Holy Spirit we mentioned before. You definitely don't want to spend good effort only to find that you forgot to plug in. You must connect to God's spiritual power grid. Start by asking God for help in effecting these changes in your life. It's as simple as taking a moment right now to call out to Him as your heavenly Father. Ask Him to bless your work, fill you with His Spirit, and show you His plans. He is waiting, and He will not disappoint.

"Call to me and I will answer you and tell you great and unsearchable things you do not know."

(Jeremiah 33:3, NIV)

Once you've made sure you're plugged in, here are a handful of action ideas that can help you make the steady progress that leads to a transformed work life. Mark the two ideas you will do this week:

☐ **Pray for three people you work with** — This doesn't have to be an intimidating task. Simply talk privately with God about coworkers and pray for His blessings and His intervention on their behalf. Which three do you choose?

☐ **Begin your day with God** — You can start small. Read your Bible; even a few verses can serve as a meaningful time with God. You may want to use a devotional to help you focus, or maybe you can read one chapter of Proverbs a day over the course of a month (there are thirty-one chapters in all).

☐ **Commit to a higher standard of work** — Decide to glorify God with your work. Produce a higher quality product or service, or do what you do with a better attitude. What specifically will you improve?

☐ **Cut out complaints** — While it can be tempting to complain in our work, it is not a part of God's will. Do you think Jesus complained while He was making tables and chairs? Identify one area that makes you want to complain. Talk to God about this one thing each day, and seek His help in developing a better response.

☐ **Go the extra mile** — If you are accustomed to doing the bare minimum required, take it one step further. Pick a new minimum for yourself that is higher than what others require of you. Now do it each day for a week.

☐ **Cultivate gratitude** — Being thankful for whatever blessings God has given you is a powerful habit to bring to work. It gives us new perspective to the obstacles and problems we face.

Say out loud what you are thankful for each hour of an eight-hour work day.

☐ **Be slow to anger** — Try reciting a Bible verse when you sense that you're getting frustrated or angry. Micah 6:8 is a good one. It tells you what God expects from you: To do justice, love mercy, and walk humbly with your God.

These are just a handful of ideas that you can use as a starting point to fight Monday Morning Atheism in the daily activities of your work. If you would like to find more ideas like these or additional resources, see the Monday NEXT Steps at the back of this book. These tools will help you with ongoing weekly reminders, assessments, and needed encouragement. It's also good to work with friends, family, or a spiritual mentor to help you identify specific habits or attitudes in your work life that God may want to change. It's important to focus on resources that pertain to your weak areas and commit prayerfully to a small action that you can do each day.

The End of a Book, the Start of a Journey

Do you remember my story of being afraid and alone in that dark hotel room? God reached out to me and let me know He was there, everywhere, in my life. He gave me new life and new purpose. Since then, He's taken me on an incredible journey.

God has a vision for your life and a divine purpose for you to experience. There is so much more available! Turn your work over to God and experience the amazing power that flows from Him through the Holy Spirit in you. You can feel alive as you face your work week. Monday through Friday, from nine to five, in overtime and in every aspect of life—a brighter future is up ahead!

As we close, I would like to share a promise God gave me during my own personal experience of finding new power in my work life. I have leaned on this promise many times over the years in my life and work. Now I would like to bless you with that same promise for your work life. He is doing a new thing in you!

"But forget all that—it is nothing compared to what
   I am going to do.

For I am about to do something new.
   See, I have already begun! Do you not see it?

I will make a pathway through the wilderness.
   I will create rivers in the dry wasteland."

   Isaiah 43:18–19 (NLT)

Thank you for taking this journey with me. My prayer for you throughout this book has been that the Lord will bless you and your work. I'm excited by the fact that you will find His peace and His joy as you continue to seek Him. Hopefully, even now, your work, especially on Monday, is starting to seem a little brighter.

Warmly Yours,

Doug

PS: Don't forget to access the Monday NEXT Steps at www.MondaySwitch.com. Enjoy your journey.

Work Life Illumination

 "Then your light will break forth like the dawn, and your healing will quickly appear; then your righteousness will go before you, and the glory of the LORD will be your rear guard." Isaiah 58:8 (NIV)

Dear God,

I am ready to live and work in Your power and truth. As I work, help keep me aware of Your empowering presence. Help me to learn how to walk and work in the power of Your Holy Spirit. I love You, Lord. Thank You for being with me in my work. Please change me from the inside out...

I am feeling so much more alive now and excited to keep learning how to experience more of God in my work. I can honestly say I have more peace and I see Him helping me through every day."
—Derek, Sales Distribution

Switch Check

☐ **Yes** ☐ **No** Do you want more of God's power to show up in your work?

☐ **Yes** ☐ **No** Is the idea of working together with God appealing to you?

☐ **Yes** ☐ **No** Are you ready for God to do something new in you and your work?

☐ **Yes** ☐ **No** Could you use more peace and a greater sense of purpose in your life and work?

If you answered "yes" to all or most these, you are ready and positioned to restore God's power to your work life.

Reflections

1) List two areas in your life at work where God might want to make renovations (e.g., attitude, character issues, work habits, etc.).

2) Can you think of a time that you committed to a change only to get derailed or quit? What was it? Why didn't it work?

3) Is God's Spirit present inside of you as your power source, giving you the ability to change the way you work? If you aren't sure, see Eternal Job Security on Page 132.

Bright Ideas

- Picture God's hand covering yours each time you turn on a light switch, start your car, or turn on your computer.

- Who do you know that would support you in this journey with God at work? Email or call him or her at a fixed time each week for the next four weeks.

- Place a battery in your workspace to remind you that God's power grid is available each workday.

Stop the Switch

You can find a new power source. Use the 5-minute Switch Quiz to find the spiritual challenges common to your work. If you haven't already, take it free at www.MondaySwitch.com.

Notes and Ideas

Monday NEXT Steps

Six Steps to God's Power on Monday

Stay Switched ON!

Switching God ON is key to fighting Monday Morning Atheism. It will take extra encouragement and ongoing use of practical tools. You'll need to form new work habits, resist old temptations, and ensure you're staying connected to God's power. We can help.

We've created the next step: THE SWITCH SIX-STEP SERIES. It helps you grow deeper through practical experience with God and helps you find ongoing purpose, peace, and power. Use tools such as the Monday Moan Meter, the Monday Text Alerts, and more, to accomplish your work and your mission. You will not work the same again.

Join with millions of others who are making The Switch a permanent lifestyle.

 Start your Ongoing Switch at work here ▶ ▶ ▶
Take These Simple Steps

THE SWITCH SIX-STEP SERIES (Book+Study+DVD+Tools)

The SWITCH SIX-STEP SERIES takes you on an experiential journey that will lead to Thriving at work instead of just surviving! It only takes 6 Mondays and 6 Steps to change your Monday work. Get started today!

 Go To: www.MondaySwitch.com

Step 1	Step 2	Step 3	Step 4	Step 5	Step 6
Monday Moan	The Switch	Wired for Work	Short Circuit	CROSSwired	MPowered

Appendix A:
About Our Research

This book is the product of ten years of research and field experience. We began this project by compiling thirty specific behavioral indicators that measure the integration of faith into everyday issues and key relationships at work. Over the last several years, we have presented this Index of On-the-Job Spiritual Health Indicators to over 5,000 Christians.

Combining census surveying of church congregations with opt-in online participation of individuals, more than 250,000 specific data points have been collected. The respondents compose a non-probability sample, but represent a highly diverse demographic profile in terms of age, gender, ethnicity, Christian faith traditions, vocational pursuits, and geography. The Index itself was crafted with the assistance of Christian experts, who helped us identify the thirty indicators that are the focus of the research.

The collected data also points to three overarching false assumptions that prevent Christians from living biblical principles at work. In *Monday Morning Atheist* we address these challenges and provide help in overcoming each.

10 Most Common Christian Work Issues
(Source: WorkLife Spiritual Health Index global report 02/2014)

- I am unable to manage my **time** without being distracted by unfocused impulses or becoming a slave to my schedule.

- I do not connect **eternal significance** to my actual work.

- I am incapable of resolving **conflict** involving office politics, gossip, slander, favoritism, and unfounded criticism.

- I do not manage **stress and discouragement** by practicing the principle of rest and recreation.

- I am not prepared to present **the Gospel** message in language that is clear, succinct, and jargon-free, yet faithful to the Scriptures.

- I am not managing all my **resources** (i.e., time, energy, talent, money) in a way that reflects God's perspective.

- I am not sure if my God-given **talents, passions, and temperament** are aligned to my present job.

- I am not narrowing my **focus** each day by setting clear limits and boundaries on my ambitions, so that work doesn't take over my life.

- I do not see my work **calling** as really serving society and God.

- I am not seeking and hearing God when making work **decisions**.

Appendix B:
About the Authors

Doug Spada

Doug's passion is helping people "Thrive at Work on Monday." He is the founder and CEO of WorkLife where he develops innovative resources to help people experience God while they work. Drawing from his unique professional and military background, Doug also speaks internationally on God's plan and purpose for our work, as well as the church's role in that plan.

As a decorated Navy veteran, he served during the Cold War onboard US Navy fast-attack nuclear submarines. He was an instructor at the Navy's top-secret nuclear training facility at the Idaho National Engineering Laboratory. Doug has received numerous commendations during his career, including an Admiral's Citation and the Navy Achievement Medal. In addition to his education in engineering, Doug has a degree in Business Organizational Management. He ran an energy consulting firm in southern California. Doug lives in Atlanta, GA, with Tricia, his wife, and their sons, Ryan and Brayden. For speaking opportunities or to contact Doug: info@worklife.org

Dave Scott

Dave is a pastor and author with a passion to help the church equip its people to serve God faithfully in the workplace. He has been involved in church planting and collaborates in a variety of other initiatives that helps him carry out this passion for missional impact.

Dave received his M.Div. from Gordon-Conwell Seminary and a Ph.D. from Notre Dame where he studied the historical roots and implications of integrating our faith and our work. He served as a missionary with Campus Crusade for Christ. Dave lives in North Carolina with his wife, Donna, and their two sons, Jonathan and Nathaniel. Contact: www.DaveScottOnline.org

Appendix C:
Acknowledgments

From Doug:

To Tricia, my friend and wife, I love you. I cherish your prayers, love, and support. My sons, Ryan and Brayden, your dad is so proud of you. To my parents, Lee and Wanda Spada, for starting me on my faith journey—I am grateful. Thank you to Rusty Gordon for serving me on this project—your friendship inspires me. Appreciation for all those who helped this book come alive, including Chuck Westbrook, Suzann Beck, and my friend Ginger Johnson. Thanks to all my coworkers throughout the years at WorkLife; you also pursued the dream of inspiring people to follow God at work. To the Theology of Work project, including Randy Kilgore, your research and service is not forgotten. Most importantly, to my God and eternal friend, thank you for giving me Your Spirit and life that produces all good things in me. You amaze me!

From David:

To Donna, Jonathan, and Nathaniel, you are the greatest blessings of my life. I want to thank those who have supported me in so many ways in my own calling, of which this project is one fruit: Ethan Pope, Steve Smith, Jones Doughton, Dave Treat, Dan Peterson, Mike Henderson, and Bill Finley. Thanks to Dr. Garth Rosell and Dr. George Marsden for making possible my historical research project on the worldview of Jonathan Edwards and the Puritans, which was the beginning of my own odyssey in understanding how God views work and calling. Thanks to my mom and late dad, Wayne and Nancy Scott, for "investing" in me. To all my siblings, I say thank you for your prayers and support. The faithful example of each of you following God has been an inspiration to me.

Appendix D:
Eternal Job Security

When Jesus walked the earth, He was in the business of transforming lives. He invited everyone He encountered to exchange their self-sufficient way of living for a new life in Him. And that offer is still valid today. (Read John 1:12.)

Your very life and even your work are rescued exclusively through Jesus and the power of the Holy Spirit; God has sent His Spirit to be with you forever and unite you with Jesus Christ so that you might become a part of His kingdom for eternity. (Read John 17:3.)

Tell God: I can't rescue even a day of my work...let alone my life for all eternity! I need you, Jesus Christ—to do this for me. (Read Isaiah 53:6a.)

Jesus, rescue me personally as I receive Your offer of Light and Life into my spirit. I believe You died on a cross for my sins and I open the door of my life and receive You as my Savior and Lord. (Read John 3:16.)

Thank You for forgiving me, giving me eternal life, and giving me Your Holy Spirit to empower and direct my life and work from this moment forward. (Read Ephesians 2:8–10.)

"Jesus said to him, 'I am the way, and the truth, and the life; no one comes to the Father but through Me.'" (John 14:6)

Appendix E:
WorkLife.org

About WorkLife.org

WorkLife's mission is to help working Christians Thrive at Work on Monday. People in every field of work can find hope, peace, and purpose in life's great mission field of work.

People benefit from:

- WorkLife's research and documented primary work issues that affect personal spiritual health at work.

- WorkLife's customized solutions that help individuals discover more purpose, balance, and peace at work.

- WorkLife's ability to partner with ministries, churches, and groups to equip and serve their members.

- WorkLife's curriculum, books, and innovative online coaching tools offered throughout the USA and internationally.

 **Visit www.WorkLife.org.**

THE SWITCH SIX-STEP SERIES
(Book+Study+DVD+Tools) All in One

Six Steps to God's Power on Mondays

The Journey begins! Interactive and personal—THE SWITCH SIX-STEP SERIES will simply and practically transform your Mondays. This interactive study leads you through an exhilarating journey of experiencing God's purpose, peace, and power in your work.

This multi-media, video-driven process includes:
- The Monday Moan Meter
- The Switch Quiz
- THE SWITCH Book
- Monday Text Alerts, and more.

It only requires 6 Mondays to SWITCH your entire work life. Designed for individual use, small group facilitation, or larger scale campaigns.

Whether you hate your job or love it, God has more for you than you imagine. His desire is for you to Thrive at work, not merely survive.

 Learn more at www.WorkLife.org.

The Switch Tool Weekly Online Subscription

How do you fight Monday Morning Atheism each week?

Interpersonal conflicts, job loss, ethical temptations, time crunches, and more.

The WorkLife Switch Tool is a self-directed, web-based system that helps people target and overcome the ever-changing issues that cause people to switch God off at work.

This tool acts as your work-week companion with powerful video clips, devotionals and quick-use tools that pack a powerful punch in a way that's easy to access. **GOAL: Staying Switched ON at work.**

Perfect for your busy lifestyle, plus creatively designed and delivered, The Switch Tool provides you with relevant teaching and help via a 2-part email/web format each week:
- **Power ON** tools for Mondays and
- **Recharge** toolbox on Thursdays.

 Visit www.WorkLife.org!

WorkLife Caffeinated

An Individual 30-week Growth Sequence

Wake Up! That's exactly what this tool will help you do—spiritually wake up. Each Caffeinated weekly segment is delivered to you via email & PDF and features:

- A situational mini story centered around a difficult work issue.
- A biblical teaching targeted to that unique work issue.
- Practical, real-life application with eternal perspective.

Reinforce your spiritual growth by taking the private mini assessment that scores how well you'd cope with that particular challenge at work. Whether it be a 1, or a 10, or somewhere in between, knowing your score can help you look for solutions and applications that will put you in a more prepared position at work. *You can't help but grow in this structured discipleship process!*

Go to www.WorkLife.org to get your work Caffeinated!

WorkLife Thrive Guides

**Biblically based studies
to help you find Life in work:**
(for Individuals or Small Groups)

This comprehensive study series targets the 30 personal work issues that cause Monday Morning Atheism. Use these case studies each with biblical guidance in a group setting or for your own personal use.

Available individually, in bundles of five, or in a single bundle of all thirty modules.

Below is a sampling of Thrive Guide topics:
The Damage of a Hectic Pace, What God Thinks of Money, Coworkers and Sex, Fighting the Wrong Fight, Answering the Hard Questions, Eternal Balance Sheet, and many more...

 Visit WorkLife.org to learn more.

WorkLife Church Guide

Mission Possible:
A Vision for Your Church
(For Church Leaders & Pastors)

Yes, it's possible to equip your people
for missions right at the point of their
greatest potential impact: their workplace!
We've spent over a decade tackling the
issue of how to empower and equip
congregations for ministry in the workplace,
and this guide gives you access to our
research and first-hand experience.

This 80-page e-guide provides the following:

- An overview of why it's essential to address workplace ministry.

- A holistic biblical framework based on six principles for teaching and
  fostering a God-filled worklife.

- Implementation ideas, best practices, and next steps.

Not on staff at your church? Buy the e-guide for your pastor or elders so
they can see the potential.

 Visit WorkLife.org to learn more.

you +

PASSING IT ON

Do you know someone suffering from Monday Morning Atheism?

Help people stop the switch at work by sharing Monday Morning Atheist in your circle of influence.

+ give away an extra copy of this book
+ virally communicate to your online networks
+ join a coworker and go through it together
+ start a five-week journey in your small group
+ share it throughout your network or business
+ inspire spiritual growth in your entire church

+ Go to *www.MondaySwitch.com* for more ideas on sharing and to order books!

Reach Your Church — Your Business — Your City

Join a select group of individuals who God is calling to champion The Switch Revolution! This is a global movement of working Christians committed to keeping God Switched ON Monday.

+ You might be the leader or possibly the catalyst that is used by God to inspire change in your entire group, church or business!

Simply take a small step and and find out now.

Investigate ways you can be a champion by visiting ▶ www.MondaySwitch.com.

Notes and Ideas

Notes and Ideas

Notes and Ideas

Notes and Ideas

Notes and Ideas